❖ ❖ ❖

Surviving the Tragic Deaths of My Children

Surviving the Tragic Deaths of My Children

God Has a Plan We Don't Understand

Charlotte Anthony

ISBN: 1544189141
ISBN 13: 9781544189147

Dedication

This book is dedicated to the one who inspired me to write—my Lord and Savior, Jesus Christ—and in memory of my beloved son and daughter.

Contents

Introduction

Death is inevitable. One day we will all come face to face with it. We do not know where, when, or how—only the Lord knows that. So we want to be ready and have our house in order.

Tragedy struck my family not once but twice. The loss of our children has been a most terrifying time for me. I did not understand this devastation or why it happened. *God has a plan I do not understand.* It took a lot of prayer and support from my church, family, friends, and relatives. I could not have made it without God's grace and mercy, his strength and comfort.

God promised he would not leave me alone. I learned to trust and depend upon his word through it all. Grief is a family affair and a process. It takes time to heal.

I know there is no more devastating loss than the loss of a child, especially when it happens suddenly. It is a heartbreak unlike any other. My loss as a mother is a different type of grief from any other loss; it's very intense.

I want people to understand that no matter what you are going through in life, in Christ Jesus, you can conquer anything. He is your source of strength, peace, and comfort. I am a living witness of what God will do. "I can do all things through Christ who strengthens me" (Philippians 4:13, KJV).

Thank you, Lord, for peace, comfort, and strength. May this life-long journey help someone else.

Chapter 1

❖ ❖ ❖

Parenting

My husband and I are proud parents of three children: Javis, the eldest; Shaun; and April. What a wonderful miracle to be able to give birth to healthy children. Thank you, Lord, for your blessings!

Javis and April were the joy of our lives from birth to adulthood. God has been with them through it all. God blessed us to nurture and take care of them. We learned to trust and depend upon God's word. We raised our children in the church, in an atmosphere of love, care, and support from our pastor and church family. My children sang in the choir and attended Sunday school and vacation Bible school. We raised them the Bible way. We trained them in the way they should go, so they would not depart from the Lord.

Of course, our children challenged us in church. They did not want to be still and always wanted to move around, just like any other child. However, through it all I learned to depend upon God's word as our children experienced life. We always taught our children to put God first, that there was nothing in life that they could not accomplish, and to set goals and follow their dreams. We also told them to never let anyone tell them what they can and cannot do. Put God first, and there is no limit!

R.I.P. Javis

Chapter 2

❖ ❖ ❖

Tragedy One— the Beginning

Javis Boe Anthony

Javis Boe Anthony, the eldest of our three children, was born January 29, 1976. As my oldest child, he was very proud. He loved sports and people. He loved to dress and look cool. His friends looked up to him as a role model; so did his brother, Shaun. He was the life of the party. He had a beautiful smile and was also smart and loving. His independence was important to him as was proving himself to others. He was a peacemaker. He loved to talk, and most of the time, he had answers to any questions.

His parents' approval was important to him; he always wanted to please us. He loved his family and always participated in family functions. He was one of a kind. He was very knowledgeable about fixing things, and he enjoyed working on cars, especially old classic cars. He grew up knowing his destiny.

I remember that as a little boy, he loved animals, especially dogs. His first dog was named Casper; he loved that dog. Casper used to get into the pool with him. Javis enjoyed music and participating in the church choir. He was a people person, a very polite young man and respectful to all adults. He also went out of his way to help others.

In preschool, he would share with the other children and always received a good report from his teacher. In kindergarten, it was basically the same thing—him sharing his toys. Most of the time, he listened to his teacher. In first grade, things changed, because he loved to talk. Through his middle school years, his worst times were due to talking in class and being distracted by whatever was going on around him. Making friends became easy because of his attitude and love for people. He had a mind of his own.

By high school, he had made a huge transformation. His life began to change because he was a teenager and thought he knew everything. His friends influenced him; his outlook on life changed. Now he was the one his friends looked up to.

At eighteen, he was the father of a beautiful baby girl, Tatiana Danae Anthony. She was the joy of his life, just as he had been the joy of our life. Although he had a responsibility, he still hung out with his friends. I reminded him on several occasions that he now had a child that needed his attention. He listened for a while but still had a mind of his own. His friends took priority, even though he loved his daughter, siblings, and his parents. He had a strong will. Tatiana eventually graduated from high school with the guidance and nurturing of her mother. She went to college and is now a role model to her siblings.

At this point, church was secondary on his list. I reminded him that God was still in control of his life and everything that he did, that God was still near to lead and guide him through. Javis listened but did not always follow through. He changed during his teen years. He listened to friends more and started hanging out with the wrong crowd. He got in trouble many times. We reminded him that God was still with him. We said, "You make bad choices, you live with it." We also said, "Warning comes ahead of destruction."

At the age of nineteen, Javis got in trouble and served time. At this point, he was no longer a leader but a follower. Again, I reminded him that until he made up his mind to follow God and his plan, his future would look very dim. God was the only one who could turn his life around, if Javis would put away his pride and ask. At this point, he had become stubborn and thought he knew more than his parents. Life began to get more complicated and difficult.

Another child, Lachelle, was born. He was excited, and Lachelle became his focus for a while. Still, his friends took priority. Then a third child was born, Javis Jr., his first son. He was happy to have a son to carry on his name. Later, there were four more children born to Javis. He named them Javison, Javshaun, Javlene, and Javaya. He loved and adored all his children. In turn, his children loved and adored him. He took time with them but not as much as I thought he should have. He would pick them up and spend quality time with them. Again, his so-called friends took priority. His life was a roller coaster. All that his children wanted was his attention, but of course that never happened.

In 2002 at the age of twenty-six, Javis was shot coming out of a nightclub. He was almost paralyzed. Again, I reminded him that God was with him, watching over him. He knew that I prayed for him every day. So he depended on my prayers to protect him while in the streets with his friends. He would say periodically, "Mom, are you praying for me?" When he got shot, the bullet missed his spine by one inch. I kept reminding him how God was continuously working miracles in his life. I told him this was a miracle. The Lord was trying to get his attention, I told him, and he was going down the wrong path.

Javis life began to change when he turned his back on the Lord. He did not want to attend church anymore and preferred to hang out with his friends. I believe he never forgot his foundation. When he decided he wanted to do his own thing—that's when life turned bad for him. One good thing about his life change was that he became interested in buying and selling cars. He had the knowledge to work on and repair them. I told him that a mind was a terrible thing to waste. But he did not like school. I again reminded him: "God has a plan for your life; all you need to do is acknowledge him." I also reminded him from time to time how God had brought him through almost being paralyzed, when he was lying in the intensive care unit with tubes in his nose, not knowing if he would live or die. I asked, "How much more needs to happen for God to get your attention? You are his property, and you belong to him; it's time to wake up." Of course, he chose to hang out with his friends. Again, I said, "Warning comes ahead of destruction. You were warned before you got shot."

Javis, my firstborn, was on my heart all the time. I loved him so much and my heart grieved for him because I knew destruction and tragedy were out there. As time went on, he got deeper and deeper into trouble, spending more and more time away from his children. My heart went out to all my grandchildren, who looked up to him as their dad. At the same time, his children did not understand what was going on with him. They loved him; that much I knew. I told Javis, "God has a plan we don't understand. He is looking out for your good even when you disobey him. He gives us chance after chance to get it right." Javis loved God and believed that he died for our sins. But he still wanted to do his own thing!

In 2012, Javshaun, who was three at the time, lived with Javis for two years. Javis took care of the child the best he knew how. This little boy is very smart and loved living with his dad. Wherever we saw Javis, we saw Javshaun as well. I would pray to God on a regular basis to watch over this little boy and protect him. God did that! My prayers were always for his protection. God watched over Javshaun until Javis's death, and he still does.

Javis's life was ended by a gunshot wound to the head on March 1, 2015. It was a horrible accidental death—there was no safety on the gun. My husband and I were devastated, and we suffered from broken hearts. We are still heartbroken and grieving for our eldest son. His life was taken at age thirty-nine—so young. He thought he had much more life to live. Again, *God has a plan we don't understand*.

The pain from the loss of Javis is intense and at times unbelievable. Often, I feel I want to do something constructive in his memory. I still think of him every day. Of course, I did not expect to outlive my son. It shattered my world and brought me to my knees.

Losing my son has changed me in a way I can't describe. My heart still hurts after a year. The agony I felt is unimaginable. My worst fear was confirmed when he passed away in the intensive care unit. I had him for thirty-nine years, and I am grateful, but it does not make the grief any easier.

Over time, I learned how to go on living. It is particularly difficult to see him robbed of reaping the fruits of his labor. I had seen him struggle for education and job security. Sometimes it seems unfair. I think about the unfinished business he left behind. He gave me money to save for his apartment. He had many dreams and plans to change his life. The sudden loss of his life left a gap that will never be filled.

Sometimes, it's difficult to accept the reality of this loss. The holidays have been very hard. Finally realizing that he will not be coming home for his birthday or a family gathering has been a challenge. It will be a long time before I feel he is gone permanently. How can I answer my grandchildren's question: "Why did Daddy die?"

I can only say, "God has a plan we don't understand."

My husband and I have assumed the responsibility of caring for Javis son Javshaun.

Thank God for strength and energy. The support of friends and family make it easier to take care of Javshaun. He is full of energy! He's having such a hard time with the loss of his dad that he is in grief counseling.

Finding compassionate friends and family has been wonderful. I cannot say it enough. All the prayers that have come forth are amazing. So much encouragement—the burden of grief is lighter when you don't have to carry it alone.

The world seems so small after the loss of my son. Hopefully, I can help someone who is experiencing the same thing. Sometimes I feel I am letting my family down, because they look to me as the strong one, and at times I feel completely inadequate. If you have not lost a child, you cannot begin to understand the pain. I know Javis waits for me at heaven's gate. My faith is all that carries me though this journey.

Even though I buried my son, I continue to count my blessings. He would not have wanted us to stop living. We must go through this period of mourning together. It was Javis wish that his parents raise his son. Thank you, Lord for a second chance!

I know that with God on my side, there is hope. Sometimes when we remember, tears fall, and that's OK. We will never be the same. After the death of my son, my focus in life changed. I had to spend a lot of time in prayer for myself. When his birthday comes around, it's tough. The last time I saw him was at his thirty-ninth birthday celebration with family; we didn't know that would be the last time.

I am blessed with eight beautiful grandchildren and love them with all my heart, but they cannot fill the void. They all hold a special place in my heart. My life is forever changed; I know that others need me. I pray that all my grandchildren be blessed through this difficult journey. I pray for comfort, strength, understanding and peace for them. I know eventually they will get over the grief.

There are many things that remind me of Javis. His smile was priceless. There are good days and bad days; they come and go. I resigned from my job because it became difficult to focus. I struggled through the day, thinking of my son. It was hard to concentrate on work while grieving. I was totally unprepared for this. But God knew exactly what was ahead of me. A few months after I resigned, we got custody of our grandson. *God has a plan we don't understand.*

Sometimes it still feels as if I am in a bad dream. My heart feels so empty without Javis. When I go out, I see people that look like Javis. The loss is not easy to get over. You learn to live with it. It's all a part of God's plan. It's all a part of going through the grief process.

I am so happy to know there is a God who understands our grief. He created a way to overcome death. I found faith to be a source of strength. As I sort out my feelings, I must be patient and wait on God. I will express my love for my son in a spiritual way.

God's Plan

"'For I know the plans I have for you,' says the Lord. 'They are plans for good and not for disaster, to give you a future and a hope'" (Jeremiah 29:11, NLT).

Happy Memories

- Javis playing basketball
- taking Javis and April on their first cruise
- April's first car, for Christmas
- our trip to Disneyland
- his smile—priceless
- Javis's dimples
- remembering his birthday
- April's delivery of her baby girl
- Javis leading his first song in youth choir
- Javis first job at Togo's
- April's graduation from high school and college
- the first prom for each of them
- April's first job at the pizza parlor

Javis's Youngest Children

Javlene and Javaya

Javlene, Age Four

The loss of Javlene's father has been very difficult for her. Initially, she still saw Javis in the house and at daycare. She always said he was waiting for Jesus. She would smile and stare and when asked who she was looking at, she would respond, "Daddy." She cries for him when upset, Just as she done since she was a baby. He was her main caretaker during the day, up until she was two and a half years old, from the time she woke up until a few hours before she went to sleep. Her world revolved around her dad. She was Daddy's girl, always at his feet. He would complain how he kept stepping on her because she was always right behind him. She truly adored her father. When she watches any movie with a princess, she refers to the prince as the "daddy." She has a lot of his personality and his ways. She still cries for him and speaks of him often, a year after his death. She states that her father taught her most of the new things she learned.

Javaya, Age Three

For Javaya, the impact of losing her father is not known yet. She was only one and a half years old when she lost him. She looks just like him—the spitting image. Javis's friends often call her his "twin." Sometimes she talks about Daddy. Often, she seems to even remember actual events, but she is so young. What will she remember as she gets older?

It has been a year. We know God does not make mistakes. He knows what he is doing. We learned to trust him because he is giving us comfort and peace. I often say that without God's grace and mercy, I would be crazy. What a tragedy in our lives! It will never be the same. I do not blame God. I thank him for giving me peace and his grace.

Grieving is hard; it affects people in different ways. For me, prayers have carried me through and are still carrying me through. The Bible says, "The prayers of the righteous availed much." There are so many people praying and giving so much support. Our dearest son Javis passed from this life. His children visit his grave on a regular basis. May he rest in peace.

6 of Javis children

Obituary

Javis Boe Anthony was born on January 29, 1976 to J. B. Anthony Jr. and Charlotte Anthony in San Jose, California. Javis attended Silver Creek High School as well as San Jose Business College.

The Anthony family joined the Eastside Church of God in Christ under the leadership of Elder Sherman Harris in 1978, where Javis actively participated in youth ministries, including the young adult (YA) Bible study classes and the youth choir known as the Eastside JCs.

Javis loved older-model cars. He was very passionate about buying and selling. Javis had hoped someday to open his own business.

He was the eldest of three children; his siblings cherished him, his children loved him, and many looked up to him. Javis was a leader with a big heart, always looking out for others. He will be missed by all.

Javis was preceded in death by his grandparents, J. B. Anthony Sr. and Ola Mae Anthony, and Charles Coleman. He is survived by his parents, J. B. Anthony Jr. and Charlotte Anthony, of Valley Springs, California; one brother, Shaun; a sister, April; and his niece, Zuri Apryl Sabree.

Javis is also survived by his eight children: Tatiana, Stacia, Lachelle, Javis Jr., Javshaun, Javison, Javlene, and Javaya of San Jose, California; his grandmother Luberta Williams of Sacramento, California; along with a host of aunts, uncles, cousins, and many friends.

R.I.P. April

Chapter 3

❖ ❖ ❖

Tragedy Two

April Sheree Anthony

It is very painful for me to write about the life of my baby girl, April Sheree Anthony, so soon after her death. With the help of the Lord, I will do this. We were blessed with a baby girl on April 30, 1982. She was so cute and precious. After having two boys, God blessed us with this bundle of joy. While I was carrying her, my husband prayed for a girl, and this prayer was granted. Thank you, Lord, for our April love. She was an intelligent little girl from infancy to adulthood. She learned to crawl, walk, and potty train at an early age. She was just plain bright and curious. April loved to eat and talk. She was the apple of her dad's eye, his April love. He loved his boys also, but there was something special about his little girl.

At the age of five, she attended kindergarten and was very intelligent; she received great progress reports from her teacher. She continued to excel throughout elementary school. In junior high school, she was recommended for the gifted and talented education program, better known as GATE. We were so proud of her. She continued to excel throughout high school. She graduated in 2000. Then she attended San Jose City College and DeAnza College, where she studied journalism and finance. April had an interest in broadcasting. She worked at a radio station for a while. She was quite capable of pursuing her many goals. She was a people person and loved being with friends. All of them were important to her. They looked up to her and respected her. She had an amazing sense of humor. April was a natural-born leader with an inspiring spirit.

Raised in the church, she loved singing in the junior choir, praise stepping, and hanging out with the young people. She was always polite and respectful. She did not like arguing or seeing people sad. She loved the Lord and attended church on a regular basis. Regularly attending church was not a problem until she moved out and lived on her own. She was reminded that God loved her and would not turn his back on her. He would always be by her side, no matter what.

In 2009 April was in a car accident on the freeway. She lost control, and the car spun out in the middle of the freeway. She ended up on the opposite side of the freeway, away from traffic. Of course, she had no idea how she got there. I told her that the Lord was watching over her, protecting her from danger, and sparing her life. I also reminded her: *God has a plan we don't understand.* Often, warning comes ahead of destruction. It can be a wake-up call. After the accident, she started going back to church a little more. Again, I reminded her, "God is giving you one more chance to get it right. You can't go through life on my prayers alone, so you must pray for yourself. God is good and so merciful. He loves us and wants the best for us.

Without him, we are nothing." I told her we are to acknowledge him doing the good and bad. She would listen to me, even when I made her go to church when she did not want to. I know she was listening to the message.

I learned from her, and she learned from me. As she became older, of course, she was the typical twenty-one-year-old—she thought she knew more than me. However, I was proud of her as she grew into adulthood. She worked while attending college and took care of herself. She had a great job. April had boyfriends, and she was concerned about whether we approved of them or not. Our approval or disapproval was very important to her. She always wanted to please her parents. We could only raise her in the fear of the Lord. We prayed she would use good judgment throughout her life and remember where God had brought her from and where he was taking her.

April continued throughout her adult life being responsible and independent. The friends she hung out with the most were girls she grew up with in church. They remained friends from childhood to adulthood. She had other friends as well, but she knew these girls all had something in common. They kept each other accountable.

April grew up to be a beautiful, independent young lady. She was a role model to her nieces and nephews. At the age of thirty-two, she became a mother to a beautiful baby girl that she named Zuri, born January 24, 2013. She was the joy of her mother's life. April was a loving mother who took very good care of her daughter. Just like her mom, Zuri is very intelligent. My daughter devoted a lot of time to her daughter and wanted to make sure she had the best in life. She taught her daughter to be respectful, as I had taught her. My daughter made sure her daughter had the best of everything. At the age of three, Zuri has certainly been affected by her mother's death. I can tell she misses her mom because she asked, "Where is mommy?" April left us to be with the Lord on May 10, 2016. Her death was caused by a head-on collision with a diesel truck. She did not suffer. She died instantly.

The loss of our son and now our daughter, all within a year—what a tragedy! This was a sudden automobile accident. Again, we are devastated and heartbroken; our baby girl is gone. I had to remember what I told my children: *God has a plan we don't understand.* We are taking one day at a time. Prayers are keeping us strong. God is giving us peace and comfort again. Without God's grace and mercy, I would be lost, depressed, and crazy. I will continue to trust God and know He makes no mistakes. The Lord is with us every day. We do not understand what is going on. What we do know is that he has everything under his control.

April's family and friends are devastated and are taking her death very hard; they are in shock. It's unbelievable! It happened so suddenly and quickly to such a young person. She had so much to live for, especially her daughter, Zuri. Tragedy is a part of life, and we don't know why it happens, but I do know that God does not make mistakes. He knows what he is doing. What is important is that we have our life in order when our time comes. God is our source in the time of need. We will not walk alone. Every morning I say, "Thank you, Lord." April is in a better place. She loved the Lord and wanted her daughter to be raised in the church, as she was.

Everyone is still taking her death very hard. We miss our baby girl. She will forever be in our heart and memory every day. I love and miss you, baby girl. God loves you more. He had another plan for your life. You will forever be missed.

I cannot describe the endless nights spent thinking about April, my only daughter. The years ahead lay heavy on my heart. Through the day, the only thing I anticipate is grief. My heart hurts. Words cannot do justice to how I feel. I keep asking God how I can get past this incredible pain.

The challenge is to learn to live with your pain, and trust that it will become less over time. Writing this helps heal the pain within. With God's help, you learn how to cope with the pain. I love my daughter dearly, but God loves her more. *He has a plan we don't understand.*

I miss my daughter every day. I am grateful for the thirty-four years we shared. She lived with me for three years after the birth of her daughter. We learned a lot from each other. She also loved to cook. She was an excellent cook and introduced us to food we had never eaten before. Oh, how I miss her. The holidays will be a challenge. She helped me a lot. I am trying to focus on the good things we shared.

I still have moments of grief, especially on special occasions. Since the passing of my daughter, I have my crying moments. I know she is with God, which makes me stop crying. It's still fresh. But I have finally accepted that she is gone.

There is not a day that goes by when I don't wake up thinking of her. I have no fear of death because I know I will see my daughter again. I also stay busy and keep my mind occupied, which does not give me time to think about her so much. She was so gifted and talented. I have a loving, strong church family; I have relatives and friends praying for my family and me daily.

I am so very thankful for God's grace and mercy. We are blessed! I am still grieving the loss of my son. I know that God has plans for us that we may never understand until we get to heaven. April was so kind, caring, and loving. She never judged others, never held grudges against those who mistreated her.

Please don't tell me you know how I feel, unless you have lost a child too. What you can tell me is that you will be there for me. I know I need to find a healthy and positive way to process my loss. I have found comfort through my daily devotion with the creator.

My faith taught me hope. God knows what is best for my daughter and me. He makes no mistakes. Who am I to question him? I pray constantly to the Lord to ease the pain and help us move on. I now look at our time together and just smile. I ask the Lord to bring her into my dreams. I'm expecting that spiritual connection.

We must remember that God does not see death as punishment. He knows that it's the next step for us, and one day we will be together again. In the meantime, cry when you need to, and scream if you must. I pray for peace and for others who are suffering a broken heart.

April was told how much she was loved. I am slowly learning to accept her death. But there are other people in my life—my husband and our son Shaun. Sometimes I fear that death will strike again. Then after a while, the fear leaves. My daughter and I were very close. She would not want me to be sad. I miss her terribly and still cannot believe she is gone.

I feel strength and peace when I ask for it. A mother never stops being the protector and arms of love for her family. I look in my granddaughter's eyes and see the pain of missing her mommy. My heart goes out to her. She said, "Grammy, Mommy is not dead anymore. I see her. She walks with me." Her daughter, Zuri, is only three years old. All of us have come together, holding each other up with each passing day.

We must all face this journey. We are only here on this earth temporarily. Death is sure to come. When April left home that Tuesday morning, I had no idea I would never see her again. I have had my share of life disappointments. "Without God, I could do nothing. Without him, I would fail. Without him, my life would be drifting like a ship without a sail."

It's a pain that I've never felt before. How does one describe the pain of a grieving mother?

The legacy of my daughter will always live on. I feel joy when I remember the laughter we shared. One of the hardest things about being a mother is holding it together when I want to break down and cry, but I can't.

Every day since the devastation of my daughter's death, my mind has been peaceful, walking with the Lord. I will never forget the moment the officer came to my door to pronounce my daughter's death. My broken heart reminds me each day how blessed I am to know the Lord as my personal Savior.

There is no justification as to why some of us must deal with tragic losses. When tragedy hits, there is no life lesson to be learned. I must remember that I am not the only mother that has lost a child. But it truly does feel as though I am the only mother. Believe me, I have tried everything to move forward. But at the end of the day, April is still dead, and it will never be OK.

My beautiful, sweet April will forever be in our hearts. I cannot get used to April being a memory. As hurt as I feel inside, I will always be grateful that my daughter graced my life. I would not trade a minute of the precious times we shared. Death cannot change that I am her mom forever. She will always be my little April love.

Now I know that God is in control; he is getting me through grief. Grieving April is not a choice—it's a reaction. There is a deep loneliness inside of me as I continue to miss April more and more. I miss her humbleness and the purpose she added to my life. April, I am always remembering you with love and will always admire the love you had for others.

My Reaction to Grief

- shock and disbelief
- overwhelming sadness
- feelings of bitterness
- separation
- intense emotions
- daily reminders
- feelings of disconnection

Every day, I talk to her as if she is in my presence. At times, I don't know how I make it through the day without her. April touched so many lives. I like to think of us walking around heaven, waiting to meet and talk to each other again.

I finally gave away most of her clothes, but I kept some. These keepsakes are a part of me that help me to go on. We all need to find the strength deep inside us to recover just a little bit of happiness. Keeping pieces of her clothing reminds me of what she looked like when she wore them.

I pray for all of us to find some peace, hope and strength in the upcoming holidays. I am looking forward to talking with family and friends and sharing the memories of our dear daughter. It will be a time of reminiscing and celebration of her life.

April and daughter, Zuri

Friends Forever

Drena, Monikka, Kenya, April, Javonne

Aryn, April and Kenya

Obituary

April Sheree Anthony was born on April 30, 1982 to J. B. Anthony Jr. and Charlotte Anthony in San Jose, California.

The Anthony family joined the Eastside Church of God in Christ under the leadership of Elder Sherman Harris in 1978, where April actively participated in youth ministries. The Sunshine Band, the Eastside JCs, the Eastside Angels drill team, and vacation bible school were only a few of April's numerous activities. From those youth groups, she developed an active social life, and many of those childhood relationships continued for her as an adult.

April attended Hellyer Elementary School and Chaboya Middle School. She graduated from Silver Creek High School in 2000. She majored in accounting at San Jose City College and DeAnza College. April developed into an independent and generous young woman. Active in many grassroots organizations, she was heavily involved with voter registration, the San Jose City College radio station, ballet, and a world dance troop.

As one of the most loving and caring people, April was always full of life, and her laughter was contagious. She was a dedicated friend, always willing to lend a helping hand. She was also a doting mother, daughter, and sister. Family was her number one priority, and she considered those closest to her to be family. A trendsetter and an authentic character, she inspired people around her to be themselves. She never judged. April accepted people for who they were. April was well traveled, as she loved to take trips with her friends and family.

On May 10, 2016, our beloved April was suddenly called home due to a tragic car accident. She leaves behind her mother, Charlotte Anthony; father, J. B. Anthony; brother, Shaun Anthony; daughter, Zuri Apryl Sabree; fiancé, Hakim M. Sabree II; and a host of family and friends. Her brother Javis Anthony preceded her in death.

Chapter 4

❖ ❖ ❖

Left All Alone
without My Siblings

Shaun Anthony

Our youngest son, Shaun, was now alone. He was without his older brother, Javis, and his only sister, April, both of whom he had loved very much. What would he do now? Javis had been his idol; they had been so close, best friends. He felt lost without him.

Shaun is still in a state of shock a year later. He is depressed and grieving hard for his siblings. "What am I going to do?" he asks. His life is not the same. He depended on his brother for just about everything. He almost did not have a mind of his own. Basically, his brother controlled his life; that's how close they were.

My message to him is: "God is your best friend. You must lean and depend on Him. You cannot go through life alone. The Lord is with you. All you must do is ask him for guidance. Everything happens for a reason. You need to function on your own."

I pray that God will encourage and motivate Shaun to get up and be responsible and make goals for himself. I have told him that he has been left alone for a reason—that it's time for him to take care of himself, pick up the torch, and go. I told him, "God will help you, strengthen you, give you peace and comfort." Friends and family are praying for him, but he should pray for himself as well. He is grieving hard and feeling alone and abandoned. I pray that God will touch his heart and let him know that he is not alone. Shaun is distant from the family. I told him that he is not the only one grieving his brother and sister.

His sister, April, played an important role in Shaun's life when Javis passed. He would call her for advice and just spend time talking to her. Oh, how he misses her! He needs to be self-sufficient and stand on his own two feet. He is still young and has a lot to offer. *God has a plan we don't understand.* I told Shaun, "He's waiting for you to reach out for his help. You are not walking this walk alone. It's time to make a change in your life." I believe everything that has happened is a message for him. Warning comes ahead of destruction. He was brought up in the church just as his brother and sister were. He knows what is required of him. Shaun knows Mom prays for him all the time, and he depends on that. I told him he needs to pray for himself, and God will help him and deliver him. He must get his pride out of the way and give God his attention by asking for his help.

He loves to hang out with his friends. He socializes with the same group of guys that Javis did. I believe his friends were touched by Javis death. I pray that through it all, they will make changes in their lives. There is a message in the death of Javis and April, a message to the unbelievers and the lost. It's time to change your lives and know that God is in control. Learn to trust God, because He knows what is best for all of us. I told Shaun, "It's real, and your siblings are not coming back. It's time to straighten up and get it together. Remember the miracle God performed, when you were stabbed seven times with a punctured lung, left for dead. God spared your life for a reason. You were left here to be an example to others and tell your story of God's goodness and mercy. It's time to stop running. You have a testimony that you can share with others of how God brought you back to life when you were stabbed and left for dead. After the paramedics got to you, they put you in a body bag, pronouncing you dead. They gave you a stimulant, and you began to move. They were in shock and in disbelief; they removed you from the body bag. That's a miracle and a testimony. Never forget what God has done for you. He has brought you from a mighty long way."

I thank God for my son Shaun and the miracle he performed in his life not once but twice. Shaun also suffered a heart attack in 2015. I believe it was from a broken heart after the loss of his brother. Again, *God has a plan we don't understand.* Just trust him. God does not make mistakes. I love my son dearly and only want the best for him. Shaun, we love you and miss that great sense of humor. You do not have to be alone and distant from your family. The Lord will never leave you nor forsake you; we are here for you. Your nieces and nephews adore you. Pick up the torch, and carry on.

The loss of a sibling is sometimes misunderstood. The focus is on the parents of the lost child. But what about Shaun? He is devastated and shocked after losing two siblings. He never imagined that he would spend the rest of his life without his brother and sister.

The emotions he feels are abandonment, fear, and anxiety. He is distant from his family; this is his way of grieving. Just because he is older does not make the pain any easier. He is easing his grief by visiting his brother's grave daily. Shaun's love for his siblings will never die. He is expressing his innermost grief by secluding himself. Over time, and with the support of others and prayer, he will heal. He shared a long history with his brother and sister.

There is no right or wrong way to mourn. You learn to mourn in your own way. The feeling of grief after death is intense in the family. Anger is a common emotion. He did not realize that the rest of his life would be spent alone. He had planned to live a successful life with his siblings. After all, he believed he would never live without them this early in life. They were all supposed to grow up together.

His brother's absence is heavy on his heart. They were so close. Shaun says, "I will miss the humor and laughter we shared. We used to joke and clown around and have fun. My brother was supposed to walk with me longer than anyone else in my life. My sister, April, the only other person who knew what it was like to grow up with our parents, was in our home. She was very supportive to me. I could talk to her at any time. There will always be a void in my heart for her, my little sister. All the hard times ahead, knowing my siblings will not be at my side, is unthinkable. There will be no one to share the joy and laughter with like my brother and sister."

I pray that Shaun's nieces and nephews remain close to him as they grow and that they enjoy the same closeness they did with their dad.

After a little over a year, the shock and grief he felt about his brother's death is slowly fading. He feels the grief creeping back on birthdays and holidays. He will always wish that his siblings were still here. Perhaps he is stronger than I give him credit for.

If you have not experienced the loss of a sibling, you cannot understand how it changes your life. The process of grief comes in many stages. Once you deal with it and get out of one stage, you then move into the next one.

Shaun knows that God is watching over him. He knows that people are praying for comfort, peace, and strength for him. He needs to spend more time in prayer, knowing that God will never leave him alone. I told him, "Never take life for granted. Live each day as if it's your last." He will survive this painful and tragic loss. He will find a way to move forward. I believe time will heal all wounds. This has been a major loss. I want him to live a healthy life.

When you are dealing with more than one loss, it will take some time. It's OK not to lose the hope and dreams you had for your siblings. There is no other relationship like the sibling connection. In an instant, your entire family life changes right before your eyes.

The impact of losing his siblings hit him on many levels. His brother was his first best friend; they shared a life together. Now it feels like his childhood never existed, because Javis is gone.

His sister died in a car accident, and he misses her so much. He is left alone, feeling a pain he has never felt before. He feels a part of him is gone, and it is so hard not to have his siblings' company, to hear their voices or see them smile. He wants so badly to feel normal again, but he is not sure he will ever fully recover from losing them.

I know that it will be OK. *God has a plan we don't understand.* Life goes on, even though right now it's hard. The support system from people that love him helps a lot. Knowing someone is praying for him makes the road easy. He is so grateful for the time he had with his brother and sister. He is learning how to let himself grieve when he needs to. He and his brother were best friends. He must express his feelings and be strong for his family and carry on. He says, "My mother is a strong woman. I can call and talk with her, and she makes me feel better."

He feels hopeless at times, unable to focus. He is fighting depression and anxiety sometimes. He finds himself questioning God: "Why *my* brother and sister?" Later, he realizes that he should not question God. God makes no mistakes. We have no idea what God's plan is or what the future holds.

Shaun finally realized that he can talk with others about his thoughts and feelings. Knowing that family and friends will listen and encourage him helps a lot. He has already been told this. "Over time, your grief will begin to soften. You will learn to get over your loss as you keep your love for your siblings alive in your heart."

At times, being left alone feels depressing for him. He must remember that depression is just a reaction and does not have to become a part of who he is. Grief is a real issue that we can overcome. I know that God promises that he will never leave me alone. I tell him, "You must be mindful, always. Depression and insecurity will control your life, if you let it."

This is a very insecure time for Shaun. Some of the best support comes from family and friends. Grief happens because we have lost someone we loved very much. It is a natural and normal reaction. The intensity of his sadness will not last forever; it will gradually get easier. The loss of his brother and sister is a deep, powerful loss.

His future depends on a successful journey through the grief process. He needs to be open and honest about his feelings; otherwise, it will be hard for him to overcome. He will be alone to gather his true feelings and look for the answers. Sharing grief as a family can be a meaningful experience for everyone involved and an important opportunity for growth.

It is a reminder that death is a surety, and we will all get there. Shaun is so thankful for the many wonderful years he had together with his sister. She was very special to him. She always had a beautiful smile, which will never be forgotten. She was a joy to others around her. He will always remember the long conversations they used to have. His siblings' legacy will live on.

Shaun is so thankful for the many years he shared with his brother. They were like two peas in a pod. Where you saw one, you saw the other. His brother was his idol; Javis taught him a lot. They always had each other's back. Javis will be remembered for the great brother he was. They also shared many difficult times. But Javis was always the life of the party. He had a great sense of humor. Even though Shaun is left alone, his brother's memory will forever be with him. Rest in peace, Javis.

Shaun is coping but is struggling on his own. There are many ways we can cope with our feelings without being alone. We can turn to our support system, which is always willing and waiting. God is always standing by. He is our most reliable support. At times, Shaun is exhausted, both emotionally and physically, from his grief. He doesn't want to let go.

I feel sad thinking of Shaun and how lonely he must be feeling. Like most of us, he has good days and bad days. I told him that he must take one day at a time. That's all he can do. Believe it or not, it could be worse. "You are in control of your life, thoughts, and memories," I tell him. "Be grateful, my son. Thank God for each waking day, which was never promised. Do not take life for granted. Be thankful for the comfort and strength that God has given you."

Shaun is in a world of his own most of the time, lost in his thoughts. When sorrow reappears, it rips him apart inside. He's trying his best to move on. The loneliness he is feeling is not easy. The hurt is tremendous, and at times, the depression takes over.

Through it all, he will learn to trust and depend on God, because God is in control of his present, past, and future.

Javis, Dad and Shaun

(sitting) Shaun, April and Javis

Grieving

Grief is a natural response to death. You may feel sad, upset, emotional, and overwhelmed. We all grieve differently. Grief can bring memories of our loved ones, which can bring some comfort.

It's not easy to help someone who is grieving. Most of the time, you don't know what to say. It's a process that takes one day at a time, with the help of the Lord and much prayer. During this time, it is important to interact with friends and relatives. It seems to make the process easier.

At times, you may become depressed and experience heart palpitations. Others' love and concern play an important part in grieving. Know that you are not alone. If it had not been for my church family and friends praying for me daily, I would be out of my mind. However, as time goes on, I get stronger. Grief is also a form of healing.

The journey through grief is not the same for everyone. We have no idea how a person feels or what's going on in his or her mind. A loss of a child is different from the loss of an adult.

No two people experience the same grief or have the same feelings. Do not let anyone tell you how to grieve—it's personal. That person might not have any idea what you are going through. How would anyone know unless that person has been where you are? It's very important that I let my relatives grieve in their own way.

I believe there is an emotional scar that will always be with you, but it does not have to take over or control your life. God is the joy and strength of my life, and I will survive with his help. Without him, I would be a wreck. Without him, I would give up. Without him, my life would be a mess. What a comfort to know that I do not have to go through this alone.

Losing a loved one is probably the most painful and difficult experience. There are so many difficult emotions that I must face.

These emotions must run their course. Writing or talking about my loss helps me heal. I can survive this. There is light at the end of the tunnel if I embrace and face the pain.

The process of healing is about more than just feelings. It is about how you think. At times, you may not accept someone's death. You may think this for a long time. You may find it difficult to think or concentrate at times. Your focus is on the person and how he or she died, or the memory of your last time together.

The grief process might take a toll on your physical health. You might get a headache, feel faint, experience chills, or feel depressed. Your behavior might change as well. You might have difficulty sleeping. You might cry when you look at photos. The grief process might require you being around others more than usual.

Sometimes you might feel the presence of your loved one or have a visual experience. At times, a dream of your loved one might be a comfort. Try not to worry if this happens to you. This is common in most cases. Some people might keep to themselves. Some want close friends around them, and others prefer being alone. It's an individual process.

Healthy grief is very important. Grief might lead to a broken heart, which will affect your health. It might also lead to a stroke. Your health is important right now; you need your strength. Despite your individual grieving process, you will discover your own pattern of dealing with your healing. If the death is sudden, you may feel a sense of shock or numbness for a while. Everything may seem unreal.

It's common to feel lifeless at times. Other emotions may occur as well. Your energy level may go down temporarily, but eventually you will regain your strength. There will come a time of renewed life. But this entire process is unpredictable. It might happen sooner than you think. I believe that grief will end with time. It must play out on its own. You cannot hurry the grieving process. Try to live your life as normally as possible. Let time take its course.

Overcoming Grief

The Powerful Word of God

"The Lord is a shelter for the oppressed, a refuge in times of trouble" (Psalms 9:9).

"Lord, you know the hopes of the helpless. Surely you will hear their cries and comfort them" (Psalms 10:17).

"Yea, though I walk through the valley of the shadow of death, I will fear no evil for thou are with me; thy rod and thy staff, they comfort me" (Psalms 23:4).

"The Lord is close unto them that are of a broken heart; and saves such as be of a contrite spirit" (Psalms 34:18).

"God is our refuge and strength, a very present help in trouble" (Psalms 46:1).

"From the end of the earth will I cry unto thee, when my heart is overwhelmed; lead me to the rock that is higher than I" (Psalms 61:2).

"In the multitude of my thoughts within me thy comforts delight my soul" (Psalms 94:19).

"This is my comfort in my affliction; for thy word has quickened me" (Psalms 119:50).

"Blessed be God, even the Father of our Lord Jesus Christ, the Father of mercies, and the God of all comfort, who comforted us in all our tribulation, that we may be able to comfort them which are in any trouble, by the comfort wherewith we ourselves are comforted to God. For as the suffering of Christ abounds in us, so our consolation also. And whether we be afflicted, it is for your consolation and salvation, which is effectual in the enduring of the same suffering which we also suffer; or whether we be comforted, it is for your consolation and salvation" (2 Corinthians 1:3-6).

I had to get a handle on my emotions. I know how important it is to stay physically fit and mentally balanced. Grief comes and goes. Coping with loss is a personal experience. I am learning to cope. There are times when my emotions take over my thinking, and I cannot function.

I must tell myself that my feelings are mine and are well within the norm. I constantly remind myself there is no right or wrong way to grieve when it comes to feelings about the loss of my children. There are times when I want to be alone, but it is important to have a support group. These individuals are a source of emotional support.

My ultimate support for overcoming grief is my relationship with Christ, knowing that he is close by, waiting to hear from me. He is teaching me how to accept and come to terms with my loss and moving forward with my life. This does not mean that from time to time I do not revisit the situation. God is so awesome. He gives me peace, comfort, grace, and mercy. The pain of my loss is real and must be felt. There will come a time when I must choose to carry on with my life. While working through overcoming the death of my children, I will come to terms with accepting my loss.

To overcome my grief, there are steps I have to take: (1) I must be patient with myself; it takes time. There is no schedule to follow. I must choose to move on and carry on with my life. (2) I must adjust my feeling of emotions. I will survive. (3) I must learn to accept what

I cannot change. I must accept a passing; I cannot bring them back. (4) I must find strength in others. (5) I must try to live a normal life. (6) The celebration of my son and daughter is important to me. I will mourn their passing for a while. The past is over, and it's time to look forward to the future. They will always be in my heart and mind forever.

Overcoming grief requires having the right perspective. I must recognize that it's a natural process. Grief serves a purpose. The feeling is only temporary. "Weeping many remain for a night, but joy comes in the morning" (Psalm 30:5).

Through it all, God is faithful. He is with us even in the valley of the shadow of death (Psalms 23:4). I can find peace in the Holy Spirit. It is a comfort that leads and guides me.

You must go through it to heal. Once you acknowledge your grief, knowing that it exists, it's more effectively dealt with.

Also, communicating openly with people whom I feel safe is therapeutic for me. My feelings on the day I buried my son were a perfect description of how I often felt.

At first, the death of my son left me empty, afraid, and bitter; death does that to those left to mourn. Few people understand the pain, the loneliness, and the frustration. But there is a God and family who understand my grief. God loves us so much that he created a way to overcome death. It was not easy. It cost God his one and only son, Jesus.

There is hope. Jesus paid the price of our sin once and for all. Because he rose from the dead, we have hope for new life, now and forever. Nothing will change the fact that we all must die. I can begin to live again because of my relationship with Jesus. It begins with prayer.

Trying to ignore the pain or keep it all in will only make it worse in the long run. For real healing, it is necessary to face your grief and deal with it. Crying doesn't mean you are weak. Showing your true feelings can help others. Crying is a normal response to sadness, but it's not the only one. There is no right or wrong amount of time to grieve. The duration of grieving differs from person to person.

To help me overcome, I think of grief as a life experience. "Grief is the price we pay for love." I did not expect my son or my daughter to die. The loss was sudden. The bad news is that you never get over the loss.

My life ended twice. I must wait until it digests. The best and most wonderful things in the world cannot be seen but are felt in the heart. Overcoming is not an easy task. It is necessary to acknowledge and work through the pain of grief, or it will manifest through some symptoms or behavior. I need to allow myself to endure the pain, to feel it and know that one day it will pass. This too shall pass.

Trusting God is the ultimate remedy for me. He holds my future and knows all about me. He is in control of how I grieve, when I grieve, and how long I will grieve. Without him, I cannot overcome what I am going through. He gives me strength and comforts me every day. He keeps on doing great things for me. Without God, I could do nothing. "What a wonderful God we serve."

I found there are things you can do to get through a time of crisis or loss:

- Be honest with your feelings.
- Allow yourself to cry, and don't hold back.
- Live a normal life.
- Eat healthy food.

- Find a support group.
- Be open with your loss.
- Communicate with family on a regular basis.
- Continue the memories and celebrate.
- Acknowledge your broken heart.

Do not let grief take over completely; it will be a disaster. Try to stay focused. You will get through this. It might take some time, but there will be a day when the grief isn't as hard to deal with. Remind yourself that the world is not over because you're going through tough times. It will still be here when you leave this world. I will make the best of the time I have. I do not take life for granted. We are here today and gone tomorrow.

I can say that life is so precious and beautiful. I will be an example to my family and others I meet. I will share with others how good God has been to my family and me. I have always been a woman of faith. I don't have to see it to believe it. It is only through God's word. What I have once enjoyed and deeply loved can never be lost, because it is a part of me. I awake each morning to start a new day, thinking about the pain of losing my children; it's forever on my mind and heart. I will not let it get me down. I go ahead and do the things I must do.

Grief is a long journey. I will not let it consume me. I can tell you that God is so merciful and loving. He gives me strength daily. I cannot say this enough. I find myself repeating this over and over because he is so awesome. He dries up my tears and lets me know it will be all right and that joy will come in the morning. I am glad that I can put emotions into words and express my feelings. I am so glad that there is a God who understands my grief when no one else does.

We are on this earth temporarily. I am happy to say that I am not afraid of death, because I know where I stand with the Lord.

To overcome begins with a prayer: "Dear Heavenly Father, please help me to find my way forward again. Do not let this grief consume me; help me, so that I may be an example to others. Please forgive me for any doubt or disbelief. Help me to find hope and joy again in your name, I pray. Amen!"

Sometimes, when you're enduring pain and the rest of the world wants to celebrate, you need to find ways to manage by yourself and get through the birthdays and holidays without your loved ones. It can be done. Each year brings new experiences and a greater recognition of how you made it through. I cannot see the future, but I know the best is yet to come. Trouble doesn't last forever.

It is not the length of time, but the depth in which you live your life. I believe it is possible to live happily ever after on a day-to-day basis. You must take one day at a time. It is only when we know and understand that we have a limited time on this earth and that we have no way of knowing when our time is up that we begin to live each day to the fullest.

I understand that losing someone you love can be very intense and hard to overcome, but it's durable. You may even feel that you will never be the same. There is no way to grieve without the pain. There are healthy ways to grieve that allow you to move forward. Do not give up on your lifelong dreams. Your loved ones want you to be happy and have a stress-free life.

You will never truly heal until you confront the loss. Allow yourself to grieve in any way that makes you feel better. When a loss is fresh in your memory, your grief deserves attention. However, you should draw the line at prolonged grieving; it is not healthy. Give yourself a time frame. Let your pain out, and let the tears flow. Do not be afraid to cry; it's normal. You will feel much better. I found myself unable to cry, even when I tried. I asked myself, "Is this normal?"

Photos of my children help me to overcome. Just because my children are gone does not mean I should not always remember them. It is comforting to know that the ties still exist. No one will ever be able to take the relationship we shared away from me. They will always be a part of me. Some mementos will always be kept to remind me of them. As a daily reminder, I have my eight grandchildren. They are the joy of my life. Some of the things they do and say remind me of their parents.

Chapter 5

❖ ❖ ❖

A Journey Full of Pain

It has been a painful journey, but I will survive. At one point, I felt emotionally and physically drained. God showed me that I could make it. I know the road is not easy, but he did not bring me this far to leave me. Lord knows I cannot make it on my own strength. I had to depend on the Lord to lead and guide me daily. He led me to lean on him in all that I do. He also gave me a sense of peace. As you know, emotional pain can bring physical stress. Heartache is a real sensation. Chest pain is common among people grieving. Worries can also be painful. Eating and sleeping are effective during this time.

The opportunity to talk about loved ones is healthy. Surrounding myself with friends and family helps to ease the pain. Often people will ask, "What can I do?" Most people want to do something to help but do not know how.

I am grateful to God for the trials that have made me stronger and drew me closer to him. I have a testimony. I have gone to a higher level in him. Thank you, Lord, for the journey you have taken me through; may it be a help and blessing to someone else. You are my refuge in time of trouble. My journey has not been in vain. There is a greater purpose.

It also helps when people listen to me. It eases the feeling of helplessness. There is always hope that life will have meaning again. I know that God has a purpose for the pain I feel. One day it will all make sense. *God has a plan we don't understand.* Hope will also bring comfort. I will find the grace and strength to go on. Again, I am a survivor. I do know that grief takes time. The journey is painful, and I will get through it with God's grace and mercy.

I must say that the intensity of the pain is so great, unlike anything I or you have ever experienced before. Your friends and relatives try to console you by saying that time will heal the pain. However, quite often, some people may carry the pain to their grave. Knowing this does not make it easier to endure the loss of a loved one. Thank God for his feeling of comfort and messages of joy.

If your loved one is taken from you suddenly, as with my daughter, do not feel that you have lost your opportunity to say good-bye. Talk to that person, and allow yourself to feel the love he or she has left for you. No matter what the relationship was prior to passing, the pain will be lifted with memories and purpose.

We all have different painful journeys, depending on our outlook on life. Some of us can lose a loved one and hold it together. There are others not quite so fortunate. When you are ready and in full control of your emotions, it's your time to release.

Sometimes the pain you are experiencing is so intense, it allows you to connect with your loved ones. Other times, it is your beliefs that prevent you from connecting with your loved ones. It's all right to experience the spiritual connection during this painful journey. It makes the journey easier. You can find your own way through this pain.

We can escape the reality of this journey. People do sometimes try to move you away from pain. Grief is not a sign of weakness, but a sign of missing your loved one. The journey weighs you down, but get up, and know that you are not alone. You are reacting to the absence of someone you love and miss, and this is normal.

While you are going through this journey, try not to isolate yourself. Let others know when you need them. This is not a time to be prideful.

Share with those who have been there. Take responsibility of your own happiness on this painful journey.

Chapter 6

❖ ❖ ❖

Recovery through Pain

Grief is a journey that we would like to avoid. It's a part of life. You never get over the loss of a loved one. It's like a puzzle—a piece of your heart will always be missing. As I try to recover, friends and family are an important part of the recovery.

The loved ones I lost are still in my heart and memories. We don't have to let go; just create a different relationship. With time, our grief journey turns into our life journey. The recovery process does not last forever. I am recovering now.

Recovery means feeling better and having fond memories. Thank you, dear God, for the memories and the walk with you through this recovery process. I'm also grateful to know that it's OK to feel sad from time to time and that talking about my loved ones is healthy.

We must take control of the pain and move forward into healing with the help of the Lord. We cannot do it alone. I pray that my journey will help someone else in a positive way. There is hope for a brighter tomorrow. May God bless you, give you peace, and comfort and heal your heart like he has done with me. Remember, grief is a process, a long journey to acceptance and healing. We must hold on to hope, and with time, things will get better. Also, remember that you are not alone; the Lord is walking this journey with you.

There is no right or wrong way to recover. I believe there will be good days and bad days on my journey to recovery.

A few things to remember as you began your recovery:

- Jesus is your source of strength.
- Memories are a must.
- The recovery process cannot be rushed.
- Your feelings matter.
- Seek stability, both mental and physical.
- Write your feelings down.
- Continue your daily routine.

No one can know the depth of your pain, and you know that you will never forget the tragedy. However, you will get through it and come back to a happy and productive life. You must keep in the back of your mind that things will eventually get better. I have made it this far with prayer. I can feel the prayers from my church family, friends, and relatives—peace and comfort come over me. Without the prayers, I have no idea where I would be. "Prayer changes things"—what a true statement that is. I am on my way to recovery every single day. Each day is different from the last. My strength has increased, and my outlook is totally different. The journey is incomplete, but the road is becoming easier to bear. With time, a change will come. This has been an amazing journey. I will survive and recover.

❖ ❖ ❖

Chapter 7

Healing Journey

My healing has come through writing, expressing my feelings, embracing spirituality, and mourning. Writing helps me through the storm, and it's therapeutic. It will take time to adjust to new circumstances. There are family and friends who give support throughout this healing process.

There are many ways to heal. You must find ways that help you. Engage in physical activity. Occupy your mind, and focus on fun things you enjoy doing. I found that having a quiet place to meditate and think of the good times with my loved ones gives me peace. Talking openly with family members helps to keep the memories alive. Keep the family traditions such as holidays, birthdays, and other memorable celebrations to help ease the pain as you go through healing. Thank God for grace, mercy, and strength.

Healing can happen in different ways. Everyone's journey is unique. Define what healing means to you, and go from there. Being able to reach out for help is important to healing.

After losing two children, the healing seems more intense and overwhelming. We expect our children to grow up and have a full and happy life. We don't expect them to leave so soon. I did not think I would outlive my children. *God has a plan we don't understand.*

There is a deep sense of loss that will always be with me. Emotions come and go. You may feel sadness, laughter, and numbness at times. You learn to take one day at a time. We have no idea what the future holds. I do know that the Lord is with me every step of the way. Turning to faith in God provides a sense of peace. Thank you, Lord.

This unique journey is designed to help me through a painful emotional loss. Healing takes place once there is acceptance. The key to surviving this healing process is hope. Those who are suffering from the loss of a child can see that others have gone through the same thing with purposeful and meaningful lives. At some point, you will find the healing tools you need to go on.

Allow yourself to heal at your own pace. It will take quite some time. What's important to remember is that your feelings are normal. There is no right or wrong way to heal. The death of my children has changed my world. While on your healing journey, you might experience a state of shock and denial, which one goes through with the death of loved ones.

Let go of expectations, take your time, and find out what works for you. Healing includes using coping mechanisms to deal with your loss. Let God carry you through the loss process to the end of the journey, until you feel comfortable.

Acceptance may mean just having more good days than bad. It is natural to feel deserted and abandoned at times. There is grace in healing. As you accept the loss, reality sets in, and your healing begins. You are becoming stronger.

The truth is that healing has no limits; an important part of the healing process is allowing oneself to experience and accept all the feelings. Everyone should define his or her own healing process. Time heals all wounds. It is a process that requires participation on your part to come to term with your feelings. One of the most important things to remember is to give yourself permission to heal.

It's time to move forward so real healing can take place. One thing you do have is control over how you prefer to heal. Another aspect of healing is that you feel good about yourself. You are in control of your healing and loss.

This loss journey is designed to help you work through painful emotions, thoughts, and memories when you have lost someone you love. Throughout my journey, the Lord is showing his divine love toward me—his comfort and strength. His loving care is always lifting me.

The process of healing also brings you to the knowledge that you are not alone. By letting go, you can begin rebuilding your life. Healing is what you think and feel on the inside. Mourning is an outward experience of thoughts and feelings. To mourn is to be an active participant in the healing journey. You will need to confront your pain and go on. Life still goes on.

On my journey, finding emotional healing has come through writing. I encourage you to keep busy doing what you enjoy. Find that spiritual place inside you.

Know that your journey will not be quick and easy. You may feel your balance is off. Acknowledge my healing:

- Acknowledge that what you are feeling is real. Acknowledge that it may take weeks, months, or years to get through this journey. You may need directions on how to proceed through these difficult times.
- Moving toward the process is difficult. It's important to express your thoughts about how you really feel. Don't hold back; acknowledge your true feelings.

- Continue to celebrate your loved ones with memories. Remember their birthday, and come together during the holidays. Recognize them as if they were still here.
- Develop a new identity. Acknowledge their presence, that spiritual connection. Part of your identity comes from the relationship you have with other people. Allow yourself to be positive, always. Others depend on you. You may feel challenged. Your deceased loved ones will always be a part of your life.
- Look for meaning. When someone you love dies, you may question the meaning and purpose of his or her life. You must come to terms with the loss. Life has its meaning in your healing journey. Move at your own pace as you recognize the hurt, and find your purpose. The healing occurs when you let go.
- Support from family and friends. You will not stop needing the support of family and friends. The prayers from my church family and friends bring me through these tough times. Prayer changes a lot of things. Support groups are necessary. God is the joy and strength in my life. He gives me strength and comfort every day. It's important that you have someone you feel comfortable with to share your feelings.

Grief Reconciled

Reconciliation is a term I find appropriate for what I have gone through. It occurs as you mourn the loss of the one you love. It's a reality, and you learn to accept what is and move on, even though it's painful. To move forward is hard, but you have to. The physical presence is not there anymore. With reconciliation come a sense of renewal and a reemergence of energy you once had. With life comes disappointment and pain. With reconciliation comes a renewed sense of energy and confidence, an ability to fully acknowledge the reality of death. Your feeling of loss will not completely disappear.

My life will move forward, and I will continue to have hope. My faith was tested, and I passed the test. All I can say is, what a mighty God we serve. Life would not be worth living without hope. I will not let disappointments rule my life and take over my destiny.

Chapter 8

❖ ❖ ❖

Journey through Loss

Loss affects all our lives. The family suffers in a tremendous way. Loss is a process, a feeling of grief and pain. I felt the terrible sense of loss from losing my son and daughter. I was shocked and devastated, separated from the ones I love who were dear to my heart. There are heartbreaking moments that cannot be explained. The pain is so traumatic, but I will get through it with God's help. It's been a year since the loss of my son and less than a year since the loss of my daughter. I miss them both very much; their love remains as I grow. The pain does lessen. Thank you, Lord.

I have hope and am grateful that God will walk with me to make the road easier. Nobody told me that the road would be easy. I don't believe he brought me this far to leave me. When we lose a loved one, there are so many emotions that come over us. By not facing the pain of loss, we place ourselves in a dark place that is not easy to come out of. If we don't face it head on, it gets more difficult to overcome.

Also, reaching out to help others helps me to heal. All of us will deal with a loss at some time or another. We mourn for our loss, but knowing that one day we will see them again gives us hope.

Through my journey, I have found peace, comfort, and healing. You can allow yourself to drown emotionally, or allow your loss to consume you physically. Or you may want to say, "God is the joy and strength of my life. He moves all pain, misery, and strife." God is my all and all. Just knowing this will help me through this journey of loss.

Just when you think your journey through grief is finally easing, here comes another trial. Each trial through life is different. We must realize that life goes on, and we must deal with every stumbling block.

I believe that God, who suffered the loss of his only son, understands our pain. He wants us to draw near to him. I hope this journey of loss will take me to another level in him.

You will need that spiritual connection. See below the problems you may face throughout this journey:

- lack of sleep
- a broken heart
- stress
- withdrawal from family and friends
- crying
- restlessness
- anxiety

We all deal with loss differently.

Chapter 9

❖ ❖ ❖

Grief Journey

Mother's Day was one of the most difficult times, with the knowledge that my two children are not with me anymore. The memories can be painful but happy as well. It's a time of quiet grief, thinking, remembering, and knowing that I had been a great, nourishing mom who loved and protected my children.

The relationship of a parent never ends. With time, coping gets better. I will always be a mother with or without my children; that will never change. I am reminded of the good times, and it helps me to grieve less. I have my faith and spiritual belief, and I know God is near.

It is during these special days we spent together as a family that I remember and recognize the joy of motherhood. With the passing of time, grief gets better. Grief and sadness can be difficult. We all grieve differently. Give yourself time to grieve; don't rush it. Be gentle with yourself, and honor the lives of those you love. Life goes on. With the help of Jesus, I am learning to cope. Allow tears to fall because it's healthy, and if you don't, that's OK too.

Recognize the stages of grief: denial, anger, and depression. At first, you might feel like you are in shock. Also, you might experience a state of depression and withdrawal. The best therapy for me was being around other people, with all the support, and knowing that the Lord is with me throughout this entire process.

Whatever grief you are experiencing is part of the process, and it does not last forever. There is no right or wrong way to feel the anger. Grief affects all aspects of your life. Some people cope better than others. Grief is different than mourning; it's more than just your feelings. Grief is the process of experiencing your reaction to the loss of the ones you loved.

With the loss of my son and daughter, each situation was different. My son was involved in a life-threatening death that I witnessed. With my daughter, it was traumatic, sudden, and unexpected. Nevertheless, they were both traumatizing and emotional experiences that I will never forget. It is important that I live a healthy life and still have connections with my grandchildren. The memories will always be alive and in my heart. My grandchildren are the joy of my life, all eight of them.

Thank God I can and will survive with all I have been through. You can as well; we need to give ourselves time to heal and grieve and know that God is with us. Without him, we can do nothing. His amazing grace will carry us through. I will move forward in my new life without my children and never forget what they meant to me.

Throughout your grieving process, you will most likely experience a range of mental, physical, and emotional symptoms. You may also feel a sense of anxiety, and a loss or increase in appetite—it varies from person to person. The stress of grieving can take its toll on your body. Don't neglect your health. You might want to think about a lifestyle change.

You might feel you want to grieve in private, without talking to people or sharing your feelings. It's all right to ask for help from others—direct family members, friends, and relatives. You cannot do this alone. A support system might be helpful. Grief counseling is also an option.

I find that consulting and talking to the Lord is good therapy for me. But do whatever works for you to help get you through the day. Praying and meditating is healthy and gives peace and comfort. Approach your belief at your pace until you find a comfortable relationship.

Grieving as a family can be therapeutic for everyone. Each person might go through it differently. My son Shaun is grieving very hard. His way of grieving is to be distant from the family. He is going through it in his own way. Giving him his space is important. I want to remain sensitive to his feelings.

You must remember to take some time to help the children. My grandchildren are having a hard time. Children are affected, just as adults are, by the loss of someone close to them. They are not equipped to deal with it like adults, but they hurt also. You can help guide children through their grief journey by talking to them; they understand more than you think they do. My grandchildren still ask for their parents.

Remember—denial, anger, and bargaining are a huge part of the grief journey. These stages help us learn to live without the ones we lost. Our hope is that with these stages comes the knowledge to better help us to cope with life and loss. The death of your loved one might inspire you to evaluate your own feelings. You may feel a sense of separation. Grief occurs in some people after they realize they are experiencing loneliness, emptiness, and isolation.

Lord, help me not to feel anger, depression, and helplessness. I also know that love never dies. We know that it is normal to feel sad for a while, but grief is often much bigger. Help me not to dwell on it, and I'll put my trust and faith in you.

A Broken Heart

You'll find comfort, guidance, and spiritual support on your journey through grief. Your soul is restored through love and faith in God. There is no one like him. He knows the beginning and ending of this journey. It is my prayer that you experience the relationship with God and know that he is your source of healing. Our hearts are broken, but we live on.

God's love will never leave you. You may feel worthless, but you are not. You may feel undeserving, but you are not. God's word is truth. We can trust him to be who he says he is. Your grief is only temporary; with time, it will heal.

We go through because we must. We also have other family members that are going through the same thing but in a different way. The pain is unbearable at times. It also feels intolerable. It seems like the pain of the world is upon you. Thank God I made it through the night.

When I lost my son, it wasn't until over a year had passed that I began to understand the deep pain that I was feeling. The pain is still difficult at times but better. I am drawn to the healing power of grief, especially grieving the losses of my son and daughter. I am beginning to feel a sense of completeness inside of me with the help of God.

I believe we all experience the trauma of loss in some form during our journey through life. It's all in how we overcome it. It can lead to more understanding of what we are going through. The grief moves through us. In giving in to our grief, we allow healing to take place. Celebrating the lives of those who died helped me focus on the wonderful memories and love we shared together.

I have become more aware of how precious life is and what it means to me. In this past year, I have grieved more. Losing my son and then my daughter was overwhelming.

No two people grieve the same. Everyone's journey is unique. One way to get through grief is to go through it head on. You will grow. You will look beyond the heartache and pain.

We know that dealing with a loss can be one of the most difficult times in a person's life. The grief of a child is a lifetime journey. My grief as a parent is a lifelong process that can be managed with the right frame of mind. It takes time for the pain to ease. I have suffered not once but twice.

My broken heart still beats after all I have been through, thank God. But nothing can stop the pain of such a difficult life. The weight of sorrow is overwhelming. When we entrust the pain of our grief to others, our emotions are weakening, and our expectations are high. We are easily disappointed when we sense that someone who loves us doesn't understand our loss. No one can comfort us like the Lord. Over time, we learn that human comfort is far from the comfort of the Lord. With people, it's for a moment; with Christ, it's for a lifetime.

God is at work in our lives to comfort us through the power of the Holy Spirit, the great Comforter. "And I will ask the Father, and he will give you another Comforter, who will never leave you" (John 14:16).

"Praise be to the God and Father of our Lord Jesus Christ, the Father of compassion and the God of all comfort, who comforts us in all our trouble, so that we can comfort those in any trouble with the comfort we ourselves have received from God" (2 Corinthians 1:3–4).

Lord, keep me in the center of your will, and continue to comfort me.

It is my prayer that God will mend your broken heart and give you peace, mercy, and grace.

Your Test: After Death

1. What are you feeling after your loss?

2. How have you been affected?

3. How are you coping?

4. How will your life change?

5. How are you coping with stress?

6. How are you processing your healing?

7. How is your health being affected?

8. What happens when you grieve?

9. What does it mean to be heartbroken?

10. What part does depression play?

11. Once you examine yourself after a death, then what?

12. What happens after death?
    - God loves us, and he has a plan for our life.

13. We all have the opportunity not to be lost. What are your plans?
    - "The result of sin is death, spiritual separation from God" (Romans 6:23).
    - Jesus died in our place so we could have a relationship with God and be with him forever.

14. What part does guilt play?
    - Guilt is painful.
    - Doubt, shame, insecurity, anxiety, and fear can come with guilt.
    - Guilt is a natural part of grief.
    - You may tell yourself, "Maybe if I had known..." or "Maybe if I had been more attentive..." Do not tear yourself down. It's out of your control. Even if I had been there, maybe it would not have made a difference. Some things are out of our control. Only the Lord knows what would have happened.
    - Grief is a part of our beliefs.

15. Are you feeling guilty?
    - The past is history and we cannot do anything about it.
    - Listen to learn how to forgive yourself
    - Your support system is an option.
    - Memories are therapy.

- Prioritize yourself and decide what you should do first.
- Take the weight of guilt off your shoulders.
- Always put God first in your life.
- Examine your spirituality.

16. Should I be guilty about enjoying life so soon?
- Remember that whatever you do, you cannot do it with your own strength. Jesus is our source.
- People judge what they see on the outside, but God sees our heart. Do not let people make you feel guilty. He is our only judge.
- Make sure before you leave this world, you know the Lord and have that personal relationship with him.

I do not want to be lost. I am looking forward to seeing my son and daughter again. Salvation is a choice. I highly recommend it. It is important to identify grief. We want peace and joy in our life. Guilt is a horrible feeling. I want to be free. Faith and your belief are critical. Hold on to your belief, and know that God is by your side, always. All you need to do is acknowledge him and let him direct your path. Also, learn to be patient with yourself. You cannot rush through life; you will only make a mess of things. Learn to live each day as if it's your last. Do not take life for granted. We do not know what tomorrow holds. My children did not expect to leave this world so soon, at such early ages.

My belief in God helps me function and accept what has happened in my life with the loss of my children. I could not have handled it alone. I would be in a dark and depressed state of mind. A broken heart can contribute to a stroke. I thank you, Lord, for grace and mercy, peace and comfort. I do not want to even think what would happen if the Lord were not in my life.

Guilt can also affect our mental and physical health. We need to keep moving and try to be as normal as possible. Exercise when you can; it helps to release stress. As we know, stress can kill you. As women, we already have a lot to do, especially if we have children. Lord knows I do not need any more stress in my life.

I am standing on the promises of Jesus. He will never leave us nor forsake us. I know he will never let me down. My faith and beliefs are strong.

I give all the glory and honor to the Lord. What a mighty God we serve. I have nothing to feel guilty about, because God is the joy and strength in my life. He moves all pain, misery, and strife. He promises to keep me, never to leave me. He never comes short of his word. We must fast and pray and keep our life clean every day. God is our all and all.

Life should be examined daily. If there is anything that needs correcting, do it right away. Never put off until tomorrow what you can do today. We do not want to repeat life's mistakes. We are supposed to learn from our mistakes. We are to be content and happy. Life is not supposed to be a punishment. It's supposed to be enjoyed.

1. Look back and ask yourself: What does it mean to be a new creature in Christ?
2. Do I deserve God's blessing?
3. Am I living a life that is pleasing to the Lord?
4. Will I be punished for the wrong I do?
5. Why do I struggle with my flesh?
6. Am I living a life that is pleasing to the Lord?

7. My sinful life is weighing me down—why?
8. What is missing in my life?
9. Do I deserve peace and happiness?
10. What can I do to turn my life around?
11. It's never too late; where do I start to begin a new life?
12. Why do we go through trials and tribulations?
13. What is God's plan for my life?
14. How do I release stress in my life?
15. How do I examine myself?
16. I want to live a life that is pleasing to God—how?
17. I want to make a change in my life before the end of the year. How do I do it?
18. Even though my life is a mess, God still blesses me. How do I show him thanks?
19. I am so grateful to God for his many blessings. I want him to know that. How do I do that? I need that connection with the Lord.
20. What should self-examination include?
    - Examine your lifestyle.
    - Examine how you treat others or interact with them.
    - Examine the words you use.
    - Examine the company you keep.
    - Examine how you pray.
    - Examine your health status.
    - You should examine your relationship with Christ. Is he pleased with your life?
    - The most important thing is where you stand with salvation.
    - When I die, where am I going? I do not want to be lost.

- Examine your relationship with your family, friends, and relatives.
- Determine whose side you are on—God's or humankind's?

21. To establish a sense of closure, what might you do?
    - Take full responsibility of your actions.
    - Grieve your loss as you wish.
    - Live your life as normally as possible.
    - Continue to celebrate your loved one's life.
    - Take care of yourself, mentally and physically.
    - Keep the memories alive.
    - Visit your loved one's grave.
    - Minimize your grief.

Chapter 10

God's Plan

People cannot see the whole scope of God's plan from beginning to end. Yet God has made everything beautiful for us. He has planted eternity in our heart. It's up to us if we want to follow God's plan for our life. The Bible is the best place to start to find God's plan. He has a perfect plan for every believer. I know God had a plan for my children. He took them at an early age. They had so much to live for, but God has his purpose and plan for them. Only he knows the future for my family and me. I know one day it will all come together. Everything is working out for my good, whether I understand it or not.

The promises of God belong to all of us. It's important that we believe it and live our life each day as if it's our last on earth. We don't want to spend our life trying to figure out God, because we never will. We are called to become what God has destined us to be. He will unveil his plan for us when it's time. We must take one step at a time and one day at a time.

The Lord already knows that we need his help constantly, so he encourages our dependence on him. When I lost my children,

I realized that he is the only one I can depend on. I wonder why so many believers are afraid to surrender their life to the Lord. Perhaps they are afraid he would ask them to do something they despise or don't want to do. Obedience to God is a must. The truth is, I don't think we will really be happy in life until we fulfill our God-given purpose. You will never find true happiness, peace, and joy until you do what God wants you to.

I thank God daily for the good and the bad, the ups and the downs. When I lost my daughter, I did not think I would ever function again, because I was hurt and heartbroken. The hurt was so painful, and her death was so sudden. It was very hard to believe that my little girl was gone. I know *God has a plan we don't understand.* Life goes on, and I keep moving. I believe everything is working for my good. We are God's workmanship, created by him. He equipped us with everything we need to fulfill his purpose.

Thank you, Lord, for your grace and mercy, and for the peace, comfort, and strength you give me daily.

If you live your life depending on God's guidance, you can count on him to lead the path of your life to a greater blessing.

Lord, I believe that you created me for a special purpose and that you have perfect plan for my life. Please completely fulfill my life for your glory. I have no other way but to lean and depend on you.

His plan is designed to bring us good, not evil. You can ask for what you want, and I believe it's God will that you will receive it. Just believe, have faith, and don't doubt. Do not try to second-guess God. I have learned to trust him in all that I do. I believe he will not put no more on me than I can bear. Continue to study God's word and pray. Prayer changes a lot of things in your life. His word is powerful with correction and training.

Listen to what the Lord is saying to you. The Holy Spirit will lead and guide you. I admit that I have a huge problem with patience. I am asking the Lord to help me; however, I must put forth the effort. Most believers desire to understand God's plan for us. We can understand by following him.

After the death of my son and daughter, I knew he was preparing a place for them and preparing me to accept his plan. Who am I to question God? He makes no mistakes and knows what he is doing. Again, I say prayer changes a lot of things. Prayer helped me when I knew someone was praying for me. Any plan he has is good. Be careful not to depend on humankind; keep your focus on God.

The perfect will of God will come to pass. His plan was established long before creation. Be steadfast, and know your destiny. I will trust the Lord until I die. He is my hope and salvation. He holds our future.

Lord, what would I do if it weren't for you? I would have no future or hope. You have been faithful to my family and me. You have worked so many miracles. You have made so many provisions for us.

I believe my loss is someone's gain. There is a lesson to be learned in all we go through. I believe someone will gain from my children's death. Hopefully someone will be saved.

Even though my heart is broken, I have a testimony of how good God is. What he's done for me, he will do for you. I can clearly see God's blessings. Yet I will serve him. He is taking me to another level in him. My faith has increased. He has given me holy boldness to be able to share his goodness and mercy with others. I have been asked many times, "Why are you so strong after all you have been through?" I can truly answer that it's because of God's grace and mercy. He keeps doing great things for me.

I will seek the Lord while he may be found. I will call upon him while he is near. He uses suffering to produce glory, and death to bring about life. No one knows the thoughts of God. We are God's children; we must live by faith, believing in things we cannot see. We must believe it will come to pass. What a mighty God we serve. He loves us so much that he gave his only son so that we may have eternal life.

Lord, continue to help me be a witness for you. Let others see you in me. I am nothing without you, can do nothing without you. We know our life here on earth is temporary. You have greater plans for us. My future is in your hands. My children's death is in your hands.

We know that death is a certainty. May our continued faith become stronger and stronger, with our knowledge that God has everything under control. May we learn to be obedient servants. May we choose to praise and please God, the perfect planner.

I have been through so much that I have no other choice but to serve God to the fullest. I pray for my surviving son because he is depressed. He will realize one day that God is his only hope and comforter. He is grieving hard right now, but eventually the pain will cease and improve with time. Right now, he cannot see that, because he is hurting from the loss of his siblings. God, promise that he never leaves us alone. My prayer is that God mends my family's broken heart. I know that it is not easy for them to move on right now.

I know God is working things out. I am leaning on the Lord's side. I keep saying to myself, where would I be without the Lord? I know God is faithful to his promise.

I love you, Lord.

I thank him daily for life, health, and strength. I know he is in control of everything that happens in our life.

The Bible says, "Trust in the Lord with all your heart; do not depend on your own understanding. Seek his will in all you do, and he will show you which path to take" (Proverbs 3:5–6, NLT). We have a God that will walk with us. God is good. God is great. Let us thank him for all things. He never disappoints us; we disappoint ourselves. He knows what our future holds. He looks out for our good. He is bigger than our mistakes. He has a perfect plan for our life.

Jesus, you are the center of my joy.

It is a privilege to be part of his plan. All that's good and perfect comes from him. There is not enough time in a day to say how good God is to me and what he has done for me. You must experience his goodness for yourself.

When life gets so heavy, weighing you down, you can go to the Lord to make everything all right. I can go to the rock of my salvation. Being saved is awesome. I live each day with joy. I do not let the problems of this world get me down, because I know without a doubt who holds my future. The world needs to know the power of God. I pray that whoever reads my book will be transformed and encouraged to the point of wanting to be saved. I want to be a witness for the Lord. I want to be used by him like never before. We are living in a trying time. The world is missing the mark. I want to live a holy life and be caught up when Jesus comes back. There is a lot I could be upset about, but why worry and stress about something you and I cannot change? Stress is a death sentence. Give all your worries to the Lord. He cares for you.

Where can I go? Who can I trust? It's the Lord himself. Time is moving so fast; there are signs of the times. Time is winding down. God is coming soon. I know that we have heard this for years. Look at this world—we are seeing things happening that we've never seen before. My husband and I will remain strong and true to God. We will not let go of God's hand.

Without God, we can do nothing; without Him, we will fail. All power is in his hands. We are going forward with our life. Our grandchildren need us now. God knew what was going to happen. He knew my husband and I would be left to raise our grandson.

They are doing so much better. They still talk about their father and mother. It's a process, and they will heal with time. They still visit their father's grave on his birthday and Father's Day, or whenever they need to. What a blessing to have him near so they can visit when they want.

I may be repeating myself; it's because I cannot say enough about God's amazing grace. I can look back and see how far he has brought my family and me. He has worked so many miracles in my children's lives. Oh, how he has blessed my husband and me through the years. The Lord has blessed us financial and spiritually. He has not failed us yet. We came this far by faith.

This book is inspired by God to help someone who may be struggling in his or her mind but can be renewed with hope. I pray that God will help the lost find their way. This is my desire. Whatever God's will is, it's for your life.

One day, when I was lost, he died upon the cross. I know the blood was for me. I am striving to get to heaven, whatever the cost. I do not want my life to be in vain. I want to live a life that is pleasing to God. We grow through life experience. "For what shall it profit a man, if he shall gain the whole world and lose his soul?" (Mark 8:36, KJV).

I want my life to be a living example. I try to let my light shine whenever I go. I want people to see Jesus in me, without saying a word. I am so glad that God looks within our heart and knows our every thought and feeling.

One question you need to ask yourself is, "Am I going to heaven when I die?" It's not about how good you are, if you go to church, or how much money you have. God says you must be born again (John 3:3). It's time to set your house in order, because time is winding down. Tomorrow is not promised

God's plan is always the best. It's trustworthy. As we sometimes face life struggles, he wants us to come to him with humility. He will be with us always. I can trust God's plan, even though I have no idea what it is. In God I trust. We can understand God's will through his word. His word is perfect.

There is no other life that I'd rather have than a life in the hand of Jesus. When I can't see my way out, he is with me to guide me, coming and going. Praise be to God. He's a wonder in my soul. It's God's plan that you be sanctified.

We can also pray that God reveals his plan to us. Draw near to God, and he will draw near to you. He's a waymaker when there is no way out. He is a mind regulator, a helper in a time of need.

I have been through a journey of pain and a journey of healing, grieving two losses, and I am still standing. Thank you, Lord; I never would have made it without you. He walks with me, and he talks with me, reminding me that I am his own.

"'For I know the thoughts that I think toward you,' saith the Lord, 'thoughts of peace, and not of evil, to give you an expected end'" (Jeremiah 29:11, KJV).

Chapter 11

Prayer Changes Things

When my son passed in 2015 and my daughter in 2016, I could not find the words to pray for myself. I called my pastor, church family, and friends to pray for me. I could feel the prayers of the people. I began to feel peace and comfort. Each day, I got stronger and stronger. Lord, thank you for answering prayers. You said, "Prayers of the righteous availeth much" (James 5:16, KJV).

Prayer changed the way I was feeling. It helps ease the pain. It made the grieving process much easier. Sometimes I just didn't know what to say. "For we know not what we should pray for as we ought: but the Spirit itself maketh intercession for us with groaning which cannot be uttered" (Romans 8:26, KJV).

I am a living witness that prayers change things. People prayed for me and kept me on their mind; they took the time to pray for me. I have seen prayer change everything in my life repeatedly. "The Lord is close to all who call on Him, yes, to all who call on him in truth" (Psalms 145:18, NLV).

When we pray, if we are still, we know that the Lord can do more than all we ask or imagine. There are many ways to pray, of course. What you say is between you and the Lord. It could just be "thank you."

Prayer can change your outlook, your circumstances, and your overall approach to life. The Lord speaks to me through the Holy Spirit, which guides me to understanding. It's important that we know when the Lord is speaking to us. Pray from your heart, and wait for the answer. He heard you. What you pray for may not come to you right away. It's on the Lord's time, not ours.

My prayer is that through the pain of loss I will know that God will continue to give me hope, comfort, and encouragement. He knows the pain of my suffering, the broken heart he is mending daily. I'm so grateful that I know him. He's done so many great things in my life. God is my refuge and strength in times of trouble.

It is so important that we take time out of our busy schedule and give God praise. At some point, we have said, "I just don't have time!" That is not true. We watch television each day. There is no reason why prayer cannot be put into our schedule. I have found that my prayer time has changed my life tremendously.

The best way to pray is to begin. The anointing will come, miracles can happen, and prayers can be answered. Also, remember that the timing of prayer is individual. Some might pray fifteen minutes, one hour, or all day. The fact that you are praying takes priority over timing. I know that sincere prayer changed a lot of things in my life.

I will take prayer over worrying any day. Give all your cares and worries to the Lord; he will work it out. Your answer will come in God's time. Please don't get discouraged if your prayers are not answered right away. God knows our heart. Just hold his unchanging hands. He will see you through every situation and pain. I have experienced the pain, suffering, and broken heart, and he is seeing me through it all.

Yet, with all that I have suffered, the almighty God is walking with me every step of the way. I trust him, because he knows what's best for me. We don't know what the future holds. I do believe that everything works out for the best. When you are going through your trials, it's hard to believe that the situation you are going through is for the best. The prayers of the righteous are so powerful. Thank you, Lord, for sending prayers my way, through my church family and friends who know you.

There comes a time in our life that we must trust the Lord in every situation. Pray without doubt, and believe that what you are praying for will come forth in Jesus's name. I am a woman of faith, and I can do all things through Christ, who gives me strength. I will not let fear rule my life. I do believe he has a plan for my life that I may never understand. What I do know is that he cares for me and loves me. If we can stay focused on the Lord and his goodness and mercy, we will be all right. I may fall, but I will get up, knowing that God is near to carry me through. What I am saying may be repetitious; that's because I cannot say enough about how good God is to my family and me. He's made ways out of no way. He keeps on doing great things for me. I am forever grateful.

Chapter 12

Conclusion

"For every thing there is a season, and a time for every matter under heaven. A time to be born and a time to die. A time to weep and a time to laugh. A time to keep and a time to throw away. A time to keep silent and a time to speak" (Ecclesiastes 3).

My life will forever be changed, but the memories will always stay with me. Eventually, with time, I will heal in my own way. I am sure at times there will be painful moments. I will not dwell on them!

Whether we acknowledge it or not, most of us fear death. We don't expect to die at an early age. Only the good Lord knows how long we will live. What's important is that we know where we are going after death. Ask yourself: did I live a life pleasing to God? Will I hear him say, "Well done, thou good and faithful servant"? Through my painful journey, I felt emotional and physically drained. I had to depend on the Lord to lead and guide me.

Each person's journey is different. Some people experience problems eating and sleeping, chest pain and worry. This painful journey will be filled with memories of my son and daughter. It's important not to isolate yourself during this process. Share your feelings with those who have been there for you. Eventually the pain will cease.

The journey of recovery leads to feeling better and having fond memories. A piece of my heart will always be missing. As I recover from my wounds, I have friends and family to get me through with prayer. I am grateful to know that it's OK to feel sad from time to time. I don't dwell on it. I must take control of my pain and move forward. There is hope for a better tomorrow. The Lord is walking this journey with me.

Loss affects all our lives. There are heartfelt moments that cannot be explained. I must remember that life goes on, and I must deal with every stumbling block. This journey of loss has given me a closer relationship with God. I will forever be grateful for all the prayers and support from family and friends.

Writing this book has been therapeutic for me. I have learned to occupy my mind and focus on things I enjoy doing. Also, I have learned to find a quiet place where I can meditate on the Lord. The loss of two children has been so intense and overwhelming. It's very difficult when the death is sudden. I will allow myself to heal at my own pace.

The relationship of a parent with his or her children never ends. With or without my children, I will always be their mother. They live forever in my heart. Do not rush the grieving and healing process. All aspects of your life are affected. Your soul is restored through love and faith in God. It is my prayer that you experience the relationship with God and be transformed through his healing.

The grieving over my son and daughter is a lifetime journey. At some point, you will look beyond the heartache and pain. Praise be to God. He is the Father of all comfort, peace, and strength. I would not have made it without the Lord. All the glory and honor goes to him. Thank you, Lord.

No one is immune to loss. This is a part of life. However, not all losses cause us to react the same way. It depends on the level of the relationship. The bond with my children will always be in my heart. The good news is that God will forever be with me in my struggle with grief. He is always with us, standing near and empowering us to conquer our fears.

Lord, I am forever grateful for this incredible journey you have taken me through, which included the healing process, the grief process with its different phases, the wisdom and understanding I've received, and the experience of learning how to acknowledge my loss. Thank you for the support and prayers of those around me. To all who read my story, may it be an inspiration to you. Know that without God, you can do nothing and that he is with you. You are not alone.

Prayer:

God, I know that you will never leave me alone.
You know what's best for me.
You do not make mistakes.
Thank you for mercy and grace.
Help me to mend my broken heart.
In Jesus's name, amen.

NOTES

My Journey through Tragedy

_____

_____

_____

_____

_____

_____

_____

_____

_____

_____

_____

_____

_____

_____

_____

_____

_____

_____

_____

_____

_____

_____

_____

_____

_____

NOTES

Healing Journey

NOTES

Journey through Loss

_____
_____
_____
_____
_____
_____
_____
_____
_____
_____
_____
_____
_____
_____
_____
_____
_____
_____
_____
_____
_____
_____
_____
_____
_____
_____

NOTES

Recovery through Pain

NOTES

Painful Journey

_____
_____
_____
_____
_____
_____
_____
_____
_____
_____
_____
_____
_____
_____
_____
_____
_____
_____
_____
_____
_____
_____
_____
_____
_____

NOTES

Grief Journey

_____
_____
_____
_____
_____
_____
_____
_____
_____
_____
_____
_____
_____
_____
_____
_____
_____
_____
_____
_____
_____
_____
_____
_____

NOTES

God's Plan

_____

_____

_____

_____

_____

_____

_____

_____

_____

_____

_____

_____

_____

_____

_____

_____

_____

_____

_____

_____

_____

_____

_____

_____

NOTES

Mending a Broken Heart

NOTES

Overcoming Grief

NOTES

Self-Examination

NOTES

Coping with Guilt

NOTES

My Journey through Prayer

_____

_____

_____

_____

_____

_____

_____

_____

_____

_____

_____

_____

_____

_____

_____

_____

_____

_____

_____

_____

_____

_____

_____

_____

_____

_____

NOTES

My Peaceful Journey

NOTES

My Comfort Journey

About the Author

Charlotte A. Anthony grew up in Laurel, Mississippi. She moved to California when she was still a teenager and met her high school sweetheart. The two have now been married for nearly forty-five years!

Anthony worked in medicine and nursing for forty-five years. Now, she is enjoying her retirement with her soul mate.

The two of them have three children but lost two to tragic accidents. Anthony wrote *Surviving the Tragic Deaths of My Children* to document her struggle to cope with this loss and encourage others who are grieving.

66713184R00058

Made in the USA
Lexington, KY
21 August 2017